Tuxedo Gin™

Vol. 3

Story and Art by

Tokihiko Matsuura

Tuxedo Gin
vol. 3
Action Edition

Story and Art by Tokihiko Matsuura

Translator/Kenichiro Yagi
Touch-up & Lettering/Adam Symons
Cover & Graphic Design/Carolina Ugalde
Editor/Andy Nakatani

Managing Editor/Annette Roman
Production Manager/Noboru Watanabe
Editor in Chief/William Flanagan
Sr. Dir. of Licensing & Acquisitions/Rika Inouye
VP of Marketing/Liza Coppola
Sr. VP of Editorial/Hyoe Narita
Publisher/Seiji Horibuchi

Printed in Canada.

Published by VIZ, LLC
P.O. Box 77010
San Francisco, CA 94107

Action Edition
10 9 8 7 6 5 4 3 2 1
First printing, November 2003

CONTENTS

Ginji Kusanagi is 17 years old and on top of the world. He just made his debut as a pro boxer and he's about to go on a first date with the girl of his dreams, Minako Sasebo. But on the eve of his date, Ginji gets into an "accident" and dies. An odd guardian angel (or perhaps it's more of a Buddhist spirit) tells Ginji about a loophole in the cycle of life, death, and reincarnation – all he has to do is live out the life of a penguin, and then he can come back to life in his former body. For Now, Ginji's settling into life as Gin-chan the penguin. But will love be ale to bloom between a boxing penguin and a beautiful girl...?

CHAPTER 1
SELLING POPSICLES!!
WOWZA!
......
ALL THESE HOT CHICKS!
What's the matter, Gin-chan?

SELLING POPSICLES!!
DIVA
HMM?
BUT MINAKO IS STILL THE BEST GIRL OUT HERE!!

CHAPTER 1
WOW! WHO KNEW THERE'D BE A GREAT BEACH LIKE THIS SO CLOSE BY?
BUT WHY DID ALL THESE GUYS HAVE TO COME ALONG?
YEAH! THIS PLACE IS GREAT!
WHAT A GREAT PLACE TO EARN A LITTLE EXTRA CASH!
IT WAS SUPPOSED TO JUST BE ME, MINAKO, AND HER FATHER-- A PLEASANT DAY AT THE BEACH...

YESTERDAY...
WHAT?! WE'RE NOT GOING TO SELL POPSICLES THIS YEAR!?
お食事処 かおる
BUT, I'VE ALREADY MADE 200 OF THEM.
AN IMPORTANT MEETING WITH SOME MARKET PEOPLE CAME UP. SORRY, MINAKO...
BUT IT'S AN ANNUAL TRADITION...
THEY'RE NOT GOING TO GO BAD. WE'LL JUST SELL 'EM HERE AT THE RESTAURANT...
手作り
.....
BUT THIS YEAR'S BATCH TURNED OUT SO WELL. THEY WOULD'VE SOLD OUT FOR SURE...
UNCLE JINGORO ...
?

HOW ABOUT I GO SELL 'EM?!
AFTER ALL, I COULD USE A LITTLE EXTRA CASH TO HELP FINANCE MY SUMMER FUN!
WELL, MUSASHI, IF YOU'RE GOING, I HAVE NOTHING TO WORRY ABOUT!
THAT SET-TLES IT!!
I'LL LEAVE EVERY-THING UP TO YOU GUYS THIS YEAR!
ALL RIGHT!!
CAN WE GO? SOUNDS LIKE FUN!
IT'S GONNA BE GREAT!
.....

OKAY, I THINK WE'RE ALL SET...
TIME TO HEAD OUT!
HEY, MINAKO.
HUH?
SINCE YOUR FRIENDS ARE HERE AND ALL, WHY DON'T YOU GUYS JUST GO HAVE SOME FUN?
I'LL DO THE SELLING ALL BY MYSELF!
BUT, MUSASHI...
BESIDES, I'M THE ONLY ONE GETTING PAID!
IT'S NOT FAIR TO DRAG YOUR FRIENDS INTO THIS.
IF MUSASHI'S NOT HANGING AROUND...
THAT MEANS ...

...I'LL HAVE MINAKO ALL TO MYSELF!!
OH, MINAKO ...
GIN-CHAN! ♡
Isn't it romantic?!
BUT IF WE WORK TOGETHER, WE'LL SELL THEM ALL IN NO TIME...
IT'S OKAY, LEAVE IT TO ME!
I ONLY HAVE ONE REQUEST...
!?

手作りアイスキャンデ
THIS IS GOING TO WORK OUT GREAT!!
.....
一本 300円
MINAKO'S HOMEMADE POPSICLES ARE THE BEST! AND IN THIS HOT WEATHER, THE GINSTER AND I WILL BE ABLE TO SELL OUT IN NO TIME!!
EASY MONEY!
HMPH!
WELL, OKAY ♫...
HE'S BEING SO NICE...
MAYBE I'LL TAKE HIM UP ON IT...
.....
..... HEH HEH HEH...
HE'S UP TO SOME-THING...

EXCUSE ME, LADIES!
!
CARE FOR A POP-SICLE? ONLY 300 YEN!!
...
一本
300円
I-IS THAT A REAL PENGUIN!?
IT'S SO CUTE
I'LL BUY ONE! BUT CAN I HOLD THE PENGUIN?!
SURE!
BY THE WAY, LADIES, MIND IF WE JOIN YOU?
BEACH VOLLEYBALL WITH A PENGUIN?! CAN HE REALLY PLAY?
FORGET IT!

HMPH! YOU'RE JUST USING ME AS BAIT TO PICK UP GIRLS.
I CAN SEE RIGHT THROUGH YOUR PLOY.
WHAT'S WRONG, GIN?
一本
C'MON NOW, DON'T SULK! THIS IS FOR THE GOOD OF KAORU RESTAURANT...
THAT MEANS WE'RE DOING THIS FOR MINAKO!
MINAKO SASEBO TOOK YOU IN OFF THE STREET. YOU *OWE* HER, RIGHT?!
FOR MI--
WE'RE DOING THIS FOR MINAKO!
一本 300円
THAT'S RIGHT! SHE'S DONE SO MUCH FOR ME, AND I HAVEN'T DONE ANYTHING IN RETURN... I MUST SHOW HER MY APPRECIATION!
...
ARE YOU SURE? WE CAN SERVE?
SURE, GO AHEAD.

SIX POINTS WINS THE GAME.
IF WE LOSE, WE'LL EACH BUY 10 POPSICLES!
REALLY? THEN, WE'RE GOING TO PULL OUT ALL THE STOPS, LADIES!!
HE SERI-OUSLY EXPECTS ME TO PLAY...
I'm a penguin, man...
BUT IF WE WIN, WE'LL SELL 20 POPSI-CLES...
HAH!
MY SPECIAL JUMPING SERVE!
NOT BAD!
RECEIVE!
SET!
!

SPIKE!!
SQUAWK!!
NICE JOB, GIN!!
.....
UNF!!
HERE WE GO!!
WHOA...
THROB THROB
...
SET!
GASP!!
SPIKE!!
SQUAWK!!
GOOD ONE, GIN!

A WHILE LATER...
WE LOST...
TEN POPSICLES EACH, AS PROMISED!
THANK YOU!!
.....
HUH?
WHAT THE--?!
AMAZING! A PENGUIN PLAYING VOLLEYBALL!!
WOW!!
A TRAINED PENGUIN!? IS THIS SOME KIND OF AN ACT?!
...

THAT LITTLE GUY'S AMA-ZING!
HEY, I'LL TAKE 6 POPSICLES!
THANKS!
THAT'S 300 YEN EACH!
HEY, LADY! I'LL TAKE THREE OVER HERE!!
YOU TALKING TO ME?!
I'LL TAKE ONE!
IT'S OKAY. I DON'T CARE IF MY BODY'S HURTING...
SHAKE
SHAKE
WE'RE IN THE MONEY!
...AS LONG AS I GET TO SEE A SMILE ON MINAKO'S FACE...
WOW, THAT WAS AMAZING!
WE'RE ALL SOLD OUT!!
LET'S PLAY ANOTHER GAME TO CELEBRATE!
ワアーッ
YIPPEE!
NO WAY!
SERVICE!
RECEIVE!
SET!
SPIKE!!
BWAP!!
SQUAWK!!

N-NO MORE...
PLEASE...
YOU SOLD EVERYTHING?! ALREADY?!
WOW, MUSASHI! YOU MUST HAVE A KNACK FOR SALES!
THAT'S RIGHT!
DARN YOU, MUSASHI ...
一本 300円
HUH?
WHAT'S THIS?

WAIT A MINUTE!
TWO PRICE TAGS?!!
一本 150円
一本 300円
I thought I smelled something fishy here...
NOW, I SEE...
I KNOW WHAT YOU WERE UP TO, MUSASHI...
THE OLD MAN GAVE YOU 200 POPSICLES TO SELL FOR ¥150 EACH FOR A TOTAL OF ¥30,000. BUT YOU SOLD THEM FOR TWICE AS MUCH SO THAT YOU COULD TAKE ¥30,000 FOR YOURSELF.
300円
¥60K
minus
150円
¥30K
equals
¥30K
Ha ha ha!
AND TO TOP IT OFF, THE OLD MAN'S ALSO PAYING YOU FOR YOUR TIME!
.....
BUT THAT'S FINE...
I EXPECT AS MUCH FROM THE GUY.
I DON'T HOLD *THAT* AGAINST HIM...
BUT!
HE USED ME AS BAIT! AND THAT VOLLEYBALL GAME!! I'M NOT JUST GOING TO LET THIS GO!!

HEH HEH...
DID SOME GOOD WORK TODAY!
BOTH RESTAURANT KAORU AND I MADE OFF PRETTY WELL.
THAT'S WHAT'S CALLED KILLING TWO BIRDS WITH ONE STONE!
AND THE ICING ON THE CAKE-- THOSE TWO GIRLS!!
I'LL GIVE THEM BOTH A CALL LATER TONIGHT!
I had a lot of fun today!
Give us a call, okay?
NOW I CAN JUST RELAX AND ENJOY THE BEACH!
THINK I'LL TAKE A LITTLE NAP...
LURK

バァーン!
.....
.....
PORTUGUESE MAN-OF-WAR
zzzz
...
PORTUGUESE MAN-OF-WAR
ペタ
ペタ
ペタ
MIKE THE GENIUS PENGUIN'S ENCYCLOPEDIA OF DEADLY AND POISONOUS ANIMALS!!
THE PORTUGUESE MAN-OF-WAR
YOU PROBABLY ALREADY KNOW THIS, BUT THE PORTUGUESE MAN-OF-WAR IS A TYPE OF JELLYFISH THAT IS VERY VERY DANGEROUS. IT'S EXTREMELY PAIN-FUL TO GET STUNG BY ONE.

TAKE THAT!
ドバチャッ!
ド!
GYAAAAAAH!!

LATER THAT EVENING ...
HMM?
WHERE DID MUSASHI GO?
?
GIN-CHAN, DO YOU KNOW WHERE HE IS?
DIVA
SHAKE SHAKE
HAVEN'T SEEN HIM IN A WHILE.
し～ん
DID HE GO HOME ALREADY...?
His stuff is gone...
MEANWHILE, MUSASHI'S EXPERIENCING A "TENDER" MOMENT.
HEY, MOM, WHAT'S WRONG WITH THIS MAN?!
UGHHH...
THROB THROB

CHAPTER 2 HUMANS...

さんさん
ミーン ミンミーン
HOW'S THIS, GIN-CHAN? DOES IT FEEL GOOD?
パチャ
パチャ
.....
お食事
電話番号

PHEW... IT'S SO HOT...
BUT... AT LEAST WE HAVE THIS INFLATABLE POOL...
Who knew we'd use it for a penguin?!
じり
じり
THE SUMMER HEAT'S PRETTY HARD ON ME. MY BODY WAS DESIGNED FOR AN ARCTIC CLIMATE.
OH NO, LOOK AT THE TIME!!
Have to open up the restaurant!
HEY, MINAKO!!
SORRY, DAD! I'M COMING!!
DON'T WORRY ABOUT OPENING UP, FOR NOW.
IT'S JUST THAT...

...I FOUND THIS GUY COLLAPSED IN FRONT OF THE RESTAURANT AGAIN.
GASP!
ぶら〜ん..
食事処
かおる
GIN-CHAN! IT'S YOUR FRIEND!!!
SQUAWK!!
MIKE?!!
チリ〜ン
WHAT ...?!

チリーン
YOU RAN AWAY? WHAT FOR?!
YOU GUYS CAN COME AND GO AS YOU LIKE FROM THAT AQUARIUM...
THAT'S NOT THE PROBLEM...
SINCE SUMMER STARTED, THEY'VE INCREASED THE NUMBER OF PENGUIN SHOWS TO 6 A DAY...
WE DON'T EVEN HAVE TIME TO SLEEP!
TWITCH
TWITCH
ALL THE OTHER GUYS ARE REALLY UPSET, TOO!!
I'VE BEEN SO STRESSED MY FEATHER'S ARE FALLING OUT IN CLUMPS!
WHO'S EVER HEARD OF A BALD PENGUIN ?!!
わ～ん
HMM...
BUT, THE SUMMER IS PROBABLY THE BUSIEST SEASON FOR THE AQUAR-IUM...
WHAT --?!
YOU TRAITOR! YOU'RE TALKING LIKE ONE OF THOSE HUMANS!!!
SQUAWK!!
MIKE! SIMMER DOWN!

HEY, ARE YOU TWO FIGHTING IN HERE?!
MINAKO ...
YOU GUYS BE NICE AND HAVE SOME WATER-MELON.
THANK YOU VERY MUCH FOR YOUR KINDNESS.
I HAVE TO GET BACK TO WORK, BUT YOU GUYS BETTER STOP FIGHTING, UNDER-STAND?
Squawk! (OKAY!)
...
IF YOU'RE SO STRESSED OUT, WHY DON'T YOU STAY HERE AND REST FOR A DAY OR TWO?
THEY'RE PROBABLY USED TO YOU GUYS BEING GONE EVERY NOW AND THEN. I'M SURE IT SHOULDN'T BE A PROBLEM...
WHAT'S WRONG, MIKE...?
SNIF SOB SOB
I-I'M JEALOUS OF YOU, BOSS...
SOB
YOU'RE SO LUCKY ...

THAT HUMAN...
SHE'S SO GENTLE AND CARING...
NOTHING AT ALL LIKE WHAT WE HAVE TO DEAL WITH AT THE AQUARIUM...
BUT YOU'RE MIKE THE GENIUS PENGUIN. THEY TAKE ESPECIALLY GOOD CARE OF *YOU*...
SNAP!
THAT'S DIFFER-ENT!!
I'm just being used!
しーん
HE'S LOST FAITH IN HUMAN-ITY...
I'VE GOT AN IDEA. BRING ALL THE GUYS TO THE OUTSIDE GATE TONIGHT!
I'LL TAKE YOU ALL TO A PLACE WHERE YOU CAN BLOW OFF SOME STEAM!!
"BLOW OFF STEAM?"

入江遊園地
AMUSEMENT PARKS AT NIGHT ARE PRETTY SPOOKY.
BUT, I GUESS I CAN'T COMPLAIN.
コツコツ
NIGHT SECURITY AT IRIE-LAND! THEY HIRED ME ON THE SPOT WHEN I TOLD THEM ABOUT MY KARATE CAREER!
THE PAY'S GOOD AND DINNER'S INCLUDED. WHAT A GREAT SUMMER JOB!
I'm so lucky...
ワッハッハ
AND I DON'T REALLY HAVE TO DO A THING!
IT COULDN'T BE...
うひひ...

MUSASHI MUST'VE GOTTEN A SUMMER JOB HERE...
GUESS IT'S JUST HIS BAD LUCK.
WE'RE ALL READY, BOSS!!
OKAY.
I FEEL BAD FOR MUSASHI, BUT WE'LL PROCEED AS PLANNED!
MOVE OUT!
HUH?
I SENSE SOMETHING FISHY AROUND HERE...
...
SHUF...

WHOA!!
入江ランド
DARK-NESS...
...MOVING IN ON ME?!
GULP...
I'M MUSASHI KONDO, CAPTAIN OF IRIE HIGH SCHOOL'S KARATE TEAM!!
YOU WON'T GET THE BEST OF ME!!

(ELECTRICAL ROOM)

WOWEEE!
IT'S BEAUTIFUL!
ぴょん!
I DON'T KNOW HOW TO TURN ON ALL THE RIDES HERE, BUT WE CAN AT LEAST GO TO THE POOL!
WE'RE GOING TO CUT LOOSE AND HAVE SOME FUN!
But, boss...
What are we going to cut loose?
Forget it...
イリエプール

(IRIE POOL)

SQUAWWK!!
THIS IS AWESOME!!
IT'S SO FUN! IT'S LIKE A DREAM!
WE'RE IN A DREAM LAND!!
I'M GLAD YOU GUYS ARE HAVING A GOOD TIME.
BUT...

ざわっ
ガヤガヤ
...I DIDN'T THINK THEY'D GO THIS WILD...
I HOPE MUSASHI DOESN'T GET INTO TOO MUCH TROUBLE...
YIKES!
.....
シュ〜...

ざわ
ざわ
WHAT HAPPENED TO YOU GUYS?! YOUR FEATHERS ARE STANDING ON END!!
DID YOU GET ELECTROCUTED?!
......
POP! POP!
UH-OH!

WOW...
BOSS, I FINALLY UNDER-STAND...
UNDER-STAND ?
IT'S JUST LIKE HOW ***WE*** WANT TO GO TO THE SOUTH POLE--HUMANS YEARN TO GO SOMEWHERE, TOO!
HUH?

BUT THERE'S NOWHERE FOR THEM TO GO...
SO INSTEAD, THEY *CREATE* THEIR DREAM WORLDS AND TRY TO ENJOY THEMSELVES...
入江遊園地
I FEEL BAD FOR THEM. IT MUST BE LONELY...
MIKE!
YOUR HEAD!!
?
YOUR FEATHERS ARE GROWING BACK!!
YOU'RE CURED!
SQUAWK!!
I *DO* FEEL MORE RELAXED!
IT'S ALL THANKS TO YOU, BOSS!
I'M HAPPY FOR YOU, MIKE!!

MINAKO!
LET'S EAT!
OKAY!
お食事処 かお
?
GIN! YOU'RE FINALLY UP!
WOBBLE WOBBLE
UGH...
.....
We were out all night...
YOU SLEPT IN UNTIL LUNCH.
YOU MUST'VE HAD A GREAT NIGHT!
Hahaha...
Look at those bags under your eyes!

入江水族館
ペンギン広場
AND NOW, LADIES AND GENTLEMEN, THE ADELIE PENGUIN SHOW IS ABOUT TO BEGIN!
(IRIE AQUARIUM PENGUIN PEN)
PLEASE WELCOME OUR LITTLE FRIENDS WITH A BIG ROUND OF APPLAUSE!
わぁ〜〜っ!!
ピッ
ピッ
ぐわっ
ぐわっ ぐわっ
THE CHILDREN...
Hurry, the penguin show is starting!
たっ
たっ たっ
THEY'RE ALL LOOKING FORWARD TO MY SHOW...
.....
AND NOW, HERE HE IS...
...THE STAR OF THE SHOW...

...MIKE THE GENIUS PENGUIN!!
CLAP
CLAP
CLAP
CLAP
RIGHT NOW, THIS IS THE BEST I CAN DO FOR THOSE LONELY HUMANS...
MEAN-WHILE...
FIRED?! BUT WHY...?
I really was attacked by some phantom of the dark...
Yeah, okay, but you're still fired!!

CHAPTER 3
A MOST MEMORABLE LURE

WOW! ATAMI SURE IS CROWDED...
WHEN IT COMES TO BEACHES, THE LIVELIER THE BETTER, I ALWAYS SAY!
BUT, MINAKO, ARE YOU SURE IT WAS OKAY FOR US TO TAG ALONG? WASN'T THIS SUPPOSED TO BE A FATHER-DAUGHTER BONDING TRIP?
OH, DON'T WORRY ABOUT IT!
DAD ALWAYS SAYS THAT VACATIONS ARE MORE FUN WITH A BUNCH OF PEOPLE!
Besides, we spend enough time together at the restaurant...
SORRY TO KEEP YOU ALL WAITING!
OH, HI, DAD--

WHAT'S WITH THE OUTFIT? I THOUGHT WE WERE GOING SWIM-MING...
HEH HEH HEH...
WE HAVEN'T BEEN HERE IN SUCH A LONG TIME, I THOUGHT WE'D GO FISHING TOGETHER JUST LIKE WE USED TO WHEN YOU WERE A KID!
.....
...
パタパタ
LOOKS LIKE GIN-CHAN IS LOOKING FORWARD TO IT...
ヒュンヒュン
BUT...

...SINCE I ALREADY HAVE MY SWIMSUIT ON, THINK I'LL GO SWIMMING WITH THE GIRLS.
B-BUT --!
NO WAY!!
THE OLD MAN TOLD ME YOU ALWAYS GO FISHING ON THE FIRST DAY!!
YOU LIED TO ME!
OH, OKAY ...
WELL...

HAVE FUN FISHING!
OKAY... DON'T STAY OUT TOO LATE...
See you later!
WAIT A MINUTE!
THEY CAN GO, BUT YOU'RE STILL COMING WITH ME!!
SQUAWK!
STRUGGLE STRUGGLE
LET ME GO, OLD MAN!! I'M GOING TO PROTECT THEM FROM PICK-UP ARTISTS!!
SQUAWK!!

HAHAHA
OUR TIMING'S PERFECT, GIN! THE SPRING TIDE IS IN TODAY, SO IF THINGS GO WELL, WE'RE GOING TO HAVE A HUGE HAUL OF FISH!
しへん
HMM ...
SULK
WOW!
SQUAWK!!
SPLASH

SQUAWK!!
GRRRRRRR!!
STOMP
STOMP
MUNCH
MUNCH
C'MON, GIN, STOP POUTING...
And stop eating up all our bait...
CRUNCH CRUNCH
I'M WORRIED ABOUT MINAKO AND HER FRIENDS...
THE BEACH IS FULL OF PREDATORS JUST WAITING TO PREY ON INNOCENT GIRLS!
I CAN'T BELIEVE IT...

IT'S BEEN OVER 10 YEARS SINCE KAORU PASSED...
DON'T EVEN KNOW HOW MUCH OF HER MINAKO REMEMBERS...
スパッ
スパッ
ボッ
!
KAORU...? HE MUST BE TALKING ABOUT...
.....
...MINAKO'S MOTHER!
ATAMI! WE ALL CAME HERE TOGETHER-- MINAKO WAS STILL IN DIAPERS...
I REMEMBER IT SO WELL...
ON THE FIRST DAY OF THE TRIP, THE THREE OF US WENT FISHING TOGETHER...

IT WAS RIGHT ON THIS VERY SPOT. I USED MY SPECIAL LURE...
I CAUGHT THE BIGGEST SEA BASS I EVER SAW...
HMPH... I'M PROBABLY THE ONLY ONE WHO REMEMBERS THAT DAY...
MAKES ME FEEL KIND OF LONELY...
OLD MAN...
HUH?
SPLASH!
LOOK AT ALL THOSE FISH DOWN THERE!
パチャ パチャ

WHOA!
LOOK AT THAT SEA BASS! IT'S HUGE!!
SQUAWK!!
IT'S OVER THERE!
スイ〜

WHERE'S MY TACKLE BOX?!
Outta the way, Gin!
SQUAWK!!
!
HERE IT IS!!
GLIMMER
MY SPECIAL LURE!
HAVEN'T USED IT IN OVER 10 YEARS!
HERE WE GO!

PERFECT CAST!
PRETTY GOOD, OLD MAN!!
HEH HEH... NO USE HIDING!
I KNOW WHERE YOU ARE!
チキチキ
HERE COMES!
GASP!
CRACK
AH...

OH NO!
THE POLE BROKE!
MY SPECIAL LURE...
A SPECIAL GIFT?
IT'S SO BEAUTIFUL... MAYBE I'LL PUT IT IN A GLASS CASE FOR DISPLAY...
DON'T DO THAT. IT WAS MADE TO BE USED.

THAT LURE IS SPECIAL ...
THAT'S NOT TRUE.
BUT IT'S HUGE... I WON'T GET MUCH CHANCE TO USE IT...
Look at the big fish...
...VERY VERY SPECIAL...
KAORU...
SNATCH!
!

WAY TO GO, GIN!!
I'LL TAKE OVER FROM HERE!
THERE'S NO WAY THAT I'M GOING TO LET THIS LURE GO!
THAT JUST AIN'T GONNA HAPPEN!!
!

NNGHH!!
!!
FWUMP
FLAP
FLAP
OLD MAN!!
THAT WAS CLOSE...
THIS LURE...
IT'S MY SPECIAL MEMENTO OF KAORU...
OLD MAN...

I TOLD HER THE LURE WAS TOO BIG TO USE...
"THIS LURE IS VERY SPECIAL, ONLY THE BIGGEST CATCHES WILL FALL FOR IT."
"THAT'S WHY IT'S PERFECT FOR YOU..." THAT'S WHAT SHE TOLD ME...
JEEZ, SHE EXPEC-TED A LOT FROM ME.
AND ALL I DO IS RUN A DINGY LITTLE DINER...
.....
BUT THEN SHE PASSED AWAY... SHE WASN'T AROUND LONG ENOUGH TO BE DISAPPOINTED IN ME.
OLD MAN...

OH MY GOSH!
WOW!! LOOK AT THE SIZE OF THAT FISH!!
MINAKO, HOW'D YOU KNOW WHERE WE WERE...?
HEY, DAD, DO YOU THINK THIS FISH IS BIGGER THAN THAT OTHER ONE YOU CAUGHT?
HUH?
DON'T YOU REMEMBER? YOU CAUGHT A HUGE FISH THAT TIME WE CAME HERE WITH MOM.
THAT WAS A REALLY BIG FISH, TOO! WASN'T IT?

OH, DAD... HOW COULD YOU FORGET?
...
I *DIDN'T* FORGET, MINAKO!
IT'S ONE OF MY MOST CHERISHED MEMORIES OF YOU AND YOUR MOTHER!
だあーっはっは
snif
...
SIMPLE, HONEST, AND UNCOMPLICATED...
AND HE PLACES HIS FAMILY ABOVE ALL ELSE...
HE'S NOT SUCH A BAD GUY...

...AFTER ALL, HE ALL BUT SINGLE-HANDEDLY RAISED THE LOVE OF MY LIFE...
民宿
潮
BUT...
WHO DO YOU THINK YOU ARE?! I'M NOT GOING TO LET YOU TAKE A BATH WITH MY DAUGHTER!!
HE'S STILL A MEAN DRUNK...
DAD! GIN-CHAN IS JUST A PENGUIN!
...
バタ
ボカ
スカ
ドカ
ドタ
Raise your flippers up higher!
カポーン
...
ごし
ごし

CHAPTER 4
I SHALL RETURN

IT WAS A HOT AND SULTRY SUMMER AFTER-NOON.
HE WAS BACK...
ミィ〜ン
ミィ〜ン
...
LONG TIME NO SEE...
ミィ〜ン
...SHIN-NOSUKE.
...
RRING
THERE WE WERE...
...THE TENSION WAS THICK ENOUGH TO STOP THE FLOW OF TIME...
RRING
......
...AND IN THAT SMALL SPACE THAT LAY BETWEEN US, HINGED THE BALANCE...

...THE BALANCE BETWEEN LIFE AND DEATH...
SHUF...
.....
PLEASE COME AGAIN!
THANK YOU!
MINAKO, SHE'S BACK AGAIN...
WHAT?

!
GASP!
HMM ...?
THE BLOODY PENGUIN MUST'VE SCARED HER OFF...
SHE DROPPED HER PURSE!
I'm sorry!
THE PERSON IN THIS PHOTO... I THINK I'VE SEEN HIM AT THE MARKET. HE'S EATEN HERE BEFORE, TOO...
OH, HE'S THE GUY THAT ALWAYS ORDERS THE DELUXE SET MENU.
HOW CAN ANYBODY FORGET THAT HAIR?!

.....
I'LL GO SEE IF I CAN CATCH HER!
SQUAWK!!
(I'LL GO TOO, MINAKO!)
HUF
HUF
HUF
OH, NO!
MY BAG ...
sigh...
OH, GOOD... I FOUND YOU!
huf huf
!
GASP!

YOU... FORGOT THIS AT THE RESTAU-RANT...
HUF HUF
OH.
.....
SNATCH
!
WHAT'S WITH THAT ATTI-TUDE?!
SQUAWK
STOP IT, GIN-CHAN!
.....
THAT PHOTOGRAPH IS REALLY IMPORTANT TO YOU, ISN'T IT?
.....

...
... SO ...
YOU GUYS WERE WORKING AT THE SAME PLACE, AND THAT'S IT?
I...
I'M NOT VERY GOOD AT MAKING FRIENDS...
...
BUT RYUTA WOULD ALWAYS TALK TO ME...
THAT'S IT...?
THAT'S ALL I NEEDED.
BUT EVEN IF HE DID COME TO OUR PLACE ONCE...
...YOU DON'T KNOW WHEN HE'LL COME BACK...
IT'S OKAY...
I DON'T MIND WAITING.
AND REALLY...
...
She's so gloomy...

...ALL I CAN DO IS WAIT.
...
SO, I DON'T MIND...
...
HEY, THIS ISN'T THE WAY HOME...
ババババ
ドドドドド
ガラ
ガラ

MINAKO! WHAT THE HECK ARE WE DOING HERE?!
.....
SQUAWK!!
IT'S GOING TO BE ALL BUT IMPOSSIBLE TO FIND HIM IN THIS CROWD...
...BUT NOT COMPLETELY IMPOSSIBLE!
I'M SORRY I DRAGGED YOU INTO THIS, GIN-CHAN.
I don't really mind but...
OKAY, LET'S START LOOKING AROUND!
Excuse me! Can I ask you a question?
MINAKO, WHY ARE YOU TRYING SO HARD TO FIND THIS GUY?

まぐろ専門
THAT GUY FROM THE PHOTO COULD BE ANYWHERE!
川鉄
WHY ARE YOU TRYING SO HARD?!
第七大通路
WE'RE NOT GOING TO FIND HIM..

I DON'T UNDERSTAND WHY YOU'RE DOING THIS IN THE FIRST PLACE...
HUF
HUF
......
ALMOST DAWN...
I'LL KEEP TRYING UNTIL IT'S TIME TO OPEN UP THE RES-TAURANT.
ズリズリ..
THERE'S STILL TIME...
I'm... I'm so sleepy...
I KNOW MINAKO IS A KIND PERSON. BUT THIS IS GOING WAY TOO FAR...
I JUST DON'T UNDERSTAND WHY SHE'S TRYING SO HARD!!
MISS! ARE YOU OKAY?
HUH...

YOU LOOK LIKE YOU'RE ABOUT TO FAINT...
!
HUH!?
GRAB
PLEASE! I HAVE A REQUEST TO ASK OF YOU!!
UMM...

THE NEXT DAY...
お食事処 かおる
...
IT SURE IS HOT TODAY... CARE FOR SOME COLD BARLEY TEA?
THANKS...
SHAKE SHAKE
You're trembling!
IS RYUTA REALLY GOING TO SHOW...?
DON'T WORRY, HE SAID HE'D COME!
PSSS PSSS
冷やし中華
CREAK
!

HEY!
LONG TIME NO SEE, KONOMI! YOU LOOK GOOD!!

KONOMI ...?
...
YAY! LUNCH IS ON US!
ORDER ANY-THING YOU LIKE!!
GREAT! I'LL START WITH THE DELUXE SET MENU!
MINAKO! WHAT'S THE BIG IDEA?!
......

PHEW ...
...
I still don't know why you went to such extremes to help Konomi out...
Ulp...
I GUESS THIS MEANS A HAPPY ENDING.
.....
I CAN KIND OF UNDER-STAND... HOW KONOMI FELT...
TAP
!
I COULDN'T HELP IT! I JUST *HAD* TO DO SOMETHING!

I KNOW WHAT IT'S LIKE...
...TO BE SEPARATED FROM SOMEONE YOU LOVE...
ALL YOU CAN DO IS HOPE AND WAIT...
!
KONOMI'S SO LUCKY... SHE GETS TO BE WITH RYUTA, NOW...
SOME-DAY...
...
FOR SURE...
I'LL BE REU-NITED WITH HIM...
GINJI...

SOMEDAY, I'LL TURN BACK INTO MY OLD SELF AND I WILL RETURN TO YOU...
...
MINAKO, PLEASE WAIT FOR ME...
BUT, UNTIL THEN...
MINAKO...
ZZZ
...I'M STUCK BEING A PENGUIN...
POUNCE

CHAPTER-5
AFTER THE FESTIVAL

HOW DO I LOOK?
お食事処 かおる
電話番号
WOW!
YOU LOOK GREAT!
AND IT FITS PER-FECTLY!
.....
REALLY?
OKAY, SEE YOU LATER!!
ドンドンドン.
カラカッカ.

ドドドドドドン
WOW! LOOK AT ALL THESE PEOPLE...
THIS YEAR'S OBON FESTIVAL IS A BIG HIT!
THE SOUND OF THE TAIKO DRUMS, THE LIGHT OF THE PAPER LANTERNS...
THE OBON FESTIVAL IS SO EXCITING...
AND...

IT'S SO GREAT TO BE HERE WITH MINAKO! IF ONLY I WAS HUMAN...
I WENT DOWN ON MY BIKE THE NIGHT BEFORE MY FIRST DATE WITH MINAKO...
IT'S A PENGUIN...
THE GOLDFISH AREN'T FOR *EATING*, GIN-CHAN...
IT'S GREAT THAT A WEIRD ANGEL HELPED ME COME BACK TO LIFE. BUT NOW I'M A PENGUIN...
IF I LIVE OUT MY NATURAL LIFE AS A PENGUIN, I'M SUPPOSED TO BE ABLE TO COME BACK AS MYSELF...
HEY, MINAKO!
?

MUSASHI!!
YOU HERE BY YOUR-SELF?
NO! I'M HERE WITH GIN-CHAN!
YOU TWO ARE ALWAYS TOGE-THER...
WHO'RE YOUR FRIENDS ...?
OH, THESE GUYS?
GOOD EVENING!
THESE GUYS ARE ON MY KARATE TEAM.
I'M KAWA-SAKI!!
I'M YASU-DA!
HEY! WHY DON'T WE CHECK OUT THE FESTIVAL TOGETHER?
SURE!

PSSST! MUSASHI!!
!
HUH?
YOUR COUSIN IS SO HOT!!
SHE SURE IS!
BUT SHE ALREADY HAS SOMEONE... SO, HANDS OFF!
SHE HAS A BOY-FRIEND...
Darn!

HAHAHA
わたあ
...
(COTTON CANDY!)
しーん
...
No cheating!
This is supposed to be fun...?
カリ
一回200円カタヌキ
OOPS!
(PAPER CUTOUT GAME!)
We didn't get a thing...
...
ヨーヨー釣り
I got one!
(FISHING FOR YO-YOS!)
HEY, LOOK AT THAT!
!

TARGET SHOOTING...
THIS IS COOL! SHALL WE GIVE IT A TRY?
DID YOU KNOW THAT GINJI'S REALLY GOOD AT TARGET SHOOTING?
300 yen a game!
WHAT!?
HE ONCE WENT 100 FOR 100.
...
IF HE SETS SOMETHING IN HIS SIGHTS, THEN HE'LL MANAGE TO GET IT. THAT'S THE KIND OF GUY HE IS.

HE'S ALWAYS DOING THINGS THAT SEEM IMPOSSIBLE.
...
THAT'S WHY I STILL BELIEVE THAT HE'S ALIVE SOMEWHERE...
MUSASHI IS GIVING ME WAY TOO MUCH CREDIT...
BUT I GUESS AN AVERAGE GUY WOULDN'T BE ABLE TO TURN INTO A PENGUIN...
TAKE YOU, FOR EXAM-PLE, MIN-AKO...
BEFORE GINJI CAME ALONG, YOU NEVER SHOWED INTEREST IN ANY GUYS AT ALL.
YEAH...

COME AGAIN!
YOU'RE GOING HOME ALREADY? HOW ABOUT WE GO GET SOMETHING TO EAT...?
I tried so many times! Why couldn't I win a single stuffed animal?
Darn it!!!
MY DAD'LL BE WORRIED IF I GET HOME TOO LATE...
.....

I WONDER WHY MINAKO'S BEING SO QUIET...
...
I...
...I KNOW SO LITTLE ABOUT GINJI...
HUH?!
I'VE NEVER SEEN GINJI SHOOTING AT TARGETS...
I'VE NEVER EVEN SEEN GINJI BOX...
I...
.....
ギュッ

I BARELY KNOW A THING ABOUT GINJI...
.....
MINAKO...
I'M RIGHT HERE BY YOUR SIDE!!
IF ONLY I COULD SPEAK...
OOF!
SQUAWK!!
KYAAA!
!

WHAT THE HELL... IS THIS GOLDFISH WATER?
I'M SORRY! ARE YOU ALL RIGHT?
DO YOU KNOW HOW MUCH THIS SUIT COSTS? WHAT ARE YOU GOING TO DO ABOUT IT?!
I-I'LL PAY FOR IT TO BE CLEANED...
UNFORTU-NATELY, THAT'S JUST NOT ACCEPT-ABLE.
!
HUH?

OH WELL, LET'S GET SOME COFFEE AND TALK THIS OVER.
UM...
NO--! I CAN'T!
NOW, COME WITH ME!
!
SOME-BODY!
!
GLINT
GINJI!! HELP!!
!
RIGHT AWAY!!

HIGH VOLTAGE FURY JAB FROM HELL!!
... GIN-CHAN ...
MR. DOKU-MAGAWA?!

WHY DO A BUNCH OF GROWN MEN HAVE TO GANG UP ON ONE LITTLE GIRL?!
THIS IS INEXCUSABLE!! I CAN'T LET THIS GO!
HOW DARE YOU?! MR. DOKUMA-GAWA HAS HEMOR-RHOIDS!
squawk!
KILL THAT THING!
STOP! LEAVE GIN-CHAN ALONE!!
SMACK!
OW!!
WHAT THE HELL?!

!?
DEFENDERS OF JUSTICE-- HERE TO SAVE THE DAY!
MU...
MUSASHI!

DAMN KIDS! THIS IS NONE OF YOUR BUSINESS!
GET 'EM!!
HEY!
WHAT THE --?!
HUH!?
...
THE PENGUIN!!
SQUAWK!!
FORGOT ABOUT ME, HUH...?
...THAT WAS A BIG MISTAKE!!
!

HIGH VOLTAGE QUINTUPLE REPEATING PUNCH!!
ARRGH!!
HIGH VOLTAGE RAPID FIRE PUNCH!!
AYAAAH!!
THAT'S ONE AMAZING PENGUIN!!
YASUDA! KAWASAKI!!
FOLLOW THE GINSTER'S LEAD!!
ALL RIGHT!
ARRGH!
SQUAWK!!

JEEZ... GOOD THING WE CAME BACK TO CHECK ON YOU. I WAS A LITTLE WORRIED, BUT I DIDN'T THINK YOU'D BE IN THAT MUCH TROUBLE!
But I sure am glad I did come back...
THANK YOU, MUSASHI.
BUT THE GINSTER SURE WAS AMAZING!
YOU ARE A ROLE-MODEL PET!!
R-really?
YOU PROTECTED YOUR BELOVED MASTER FROM DANGER...
YOU MUST REALLY LOVE MINAKO.
TOO BAD YOU'RE JUST A PENGUIN...
Sob.

NOT THAT IT MATTERS. AFTER ALL, MINAKO ONLY HAS EYES FOR GINJI!
ワーーーッハッハッ
しーん
OOPS...
S-SORRY MINAKO... I DIDN'T MEAN TO--
HUH?
GASP
OH...!
IT'S OKAY!
I WAS JUST THINKING ABOUT GINJI...
ABOUT ME?!
かお
か

YOU SEE...
I DON'T KNOW ALL THAT MUCH ABOUT GINJI... SO I WAS TRYING TO IMAGINE WHAT HE'S LIKE...
I HEAR ABOUT HIM FROM YOU, MUSASHI...
AND THEN SHOSUKE AND GINJI'S COACH...
THEY TOLD ME WHAT GINJI THE BOXER IS LIKE...
GINJI HAS MANY GREAT FRIENDS...
HM...
IT MAKES ME WANT TO MEET HIM EVEN MORE!
MINAKO!!
IF...
...HE WERE HERE ...

...THERE'D BE SO MUCH I'D WANT TO TELL HIM!!
...AND I'D WANT HIM TO TELL ME EVERY-THING ABOUT HIMSELF!!
YEAH! AND THAT'S WHY HE'S SURE TO COME BACK TO YOU!
...
UH-HUH...

WHERE EVER HE IS, GINJI IS PROBABLY LOOKING AT THIS VERY SAME MOON...
...AND HE'S PROBABLY THINKING ABOUT US...
SURE...
MINAKO AND MUSASHI HAD ABSO-LUTELY NO IDEA...
...BUT I'M RIGHT HERE...
Minako...
...THAT GINJI WAS RIGHT THERE, LOOKING AT THE MOON WITH THEM...

CHAPTER-6
FLIGHT!

かおる
ガタガタ
TYPHOON...
I'M SHUT IN THE HOUSE, ENCLOSED WITHIN... AN OMINOUS FEELING HANGS IN THE AIR...
I'M ALONE IN THIS HOUSE WITH...
MEOW
HIM...

ゴロゴロ
.....
SHIN-NO-SUKE ... DAMN YOU!
HOW MANY TIMES HAVE I TOLD YOU...?!
MEOW
SQUAWK!!
STOP STALKING ME!!
I'M NOT GOING TO BE YOUR PREY!!
UMF!!
I'M HOME!
IT'S MINAKO! I'M SAFE!
...
MINAKO! I'M SO GLAD YOU'RE HOME!
スタ

I JUST HAVE TO DO SOME-THING...
HUH?!
MINAKO! SHINNOSUKE ALMOST GOT ME, JUST NOW...
MINAKO! WHAT'S THE MATTER?
MINAKO ...?
...?
Minako's ignoring me...
...

OKAY!
WAIT A MINUTE, MINAKO!!
YOU'RE NOT GOING TO TIE SHIN-NOSUKE UP WITH THAT, ARE YOU?!
That would be excessive force!
HAVE TO GO...
HUH?
BUT THE TYPHOON...
WHY ARE YOU GOING OUT AGAIN IN THIS WEATHER?!
MINAKO!!
お食事処

ゴオォオオォ
ヒュ
(FEMALES PROHIBITED!! DANSHOKU HIGH SCHOOL)
女人禁制!!
私立男色高校
オォォ
......
DANSHOKU HIGH SCHOOL?! THIS BOYS SCHOOL IS FAMOUS FOR ITS ATHLETICS PROGRAM ...
AND GUYS FROM DANSHOKU ALWAYS SEEM TO GET ALL THE GIRLS-- ESPECIALLY GIRLS FROM IRIE HIGH!!
WAIT A MINUTE...
FWOOSH

Sorry, Ginji! I have a new boy-friend!
HAS SHE FALLEN FOR THEIR CONNIVING TRICKERY?!
BUT I'M JUST A PENGUIN... I DON'T HAVE ANY RIGHT TO INTERFERE.
.....
Hmph!
.....
GINJI KUSANAGI! STOP BEING SO SELFISH!
IF MINAKO DECIDES TO GO OUT WITH ANOTHER GUY, I SWORE NOT TO INTERFERE!
I SHOULD TAKE IT LIKE A MAN AND BE HAPPY FOR MINAKO!
BUT I'M NOT A MAN! I'M A PENGUIN... sob...

ビュウゥ
I THINK IT'S SOME-WHERE AROUND HERE...
HUH?
BUT THIS IS...

...SEWER DRAIN OFF?
I SAW IT FROM THE OTHER SIDE, BUT I THINK THIS IS THE PLACE...
Rendezvous by sewage? Not very romantic...
!
GIN-CHAN, WHAT ARE YOU DOING HERE?!
You shouldn't be out in this typhoon!!
YOU JUST NOTICED THAT I'M HERE...?
!?
Meow...

MEOW...
THERE IT IS!!
HANG ON! I'M GOING TO RESCUE YOU!!
YIKES! IT'S A CAT!!
SQUAWK!
だあっ!
WHAT!?
HUH?!
RESCUE?
WAIT A MINUTE ...
FWIP
How's she going to get down there?

HERE I GO!
SQUAWK!!
シャキッ!
MINAKO, WHAT ARE YOU DOING?!
You could get hurt!
!
HEY!
LET GO, GIN-CHAN!!
IF THIS RIVER KEEPS RISING, THAT LITTLE CAT WILL DROWN!
I *HAVE* TO SAVE IT!!
I CAN'T CHANGE HER MIND. I HAVE TO DO SOME-THING...
...
.....

.....
IT'S SO FAR DOWN!
AND I'M AFRAID OF CATS, TOO!!
ULP...
Meow
BUT I CAN'T LET MINAKO DO THIS!!
.....
GIN-CHAN! WHAT ARE YOU DOING?!
AND BESIDES...
GASP!

...PENGUINS ARE BIRDS, TOO!!
IF IT'S FOR MINAKO...
I'LL TRY TO FLY IN THE SKY!!
GIN-CHAN, NO!!
FLAP FLAP FLAP FLAP
!

NOOOOO!
I'M NOT FLYING...
WHOOOOSH!

WHOOSH
!?
HUH ...?!
I'M FLYING...
BUT... I'M A PENGUIN...

I'M...
I'M ALIVE...
...
IF THAT HUGE GUST OF WIND HADN'T BLOWN ME BACK UP HERE...
I WOULD HAVE BEEN TOAST...
GIN-CHAN...
...?
YOU IDIOT!!
SLAP!
OUCH!
HUH?

HOW COULD YOU BE SO RECKLESS?!
IT'S A MIRACLE THAT YOU SURVIVED!
...
I KNOW YOU WERE WORRIED ABOUT ME... BUT WHAT WOULD'VE HAPPENED IF YOU DIED?!
WHAT WOULD I DO?!
MINAKO...
I'M SORRY...

THE NEXT DAY...
The Calm After the Storm!
ミィーン
ミィーン
ねろ
RRING
...
...
チリーン..
PTEW!
FLOP
SHINNO-SUKE...
SO THAT CAT WAS YOUR GIRL-FRIEND...
MEOW...
チリーン...
A gecko...
Guess he's trying to show his grati-tude...

CHAPTER 7
ALL ABOUT PENGUINS

MORNING AT RES-TAURANT KAORU...
PHEW...
IT'S GOING TO BE ANOTHER HOT ONE AGAIN TODAY. HOW ARE YOU HOLDING UP, GIN-CHAN?
Sigh...
SCAN SCAN
......
NO SIGN OF SHINNOSUKE...

SHINNOSUKE'S BEEN PUTTING ON THE PRESSURE LATELY. HE'S BEEN HUNTING ME DOWN FOR DAYS!
You're looking tasty, meow...
チリーン
SHINNOSUKE
HAVEN'T SEEN HIM TODAY...
BUT...
...
かおる
I KNOW HE'S STALKING ME!
HE WILL COME FOR SURE...
ザッ
ズザッ!
WHERE ARE YOU?!
THERE IT IS!!
SQUAWK!!

IT'S A HUGE SWALLOW-TAIL BUTTERFLY!!
だぁっ!
GET IT!!
だぁ〜っ!
...
.....
ヒュ
ウゥ...
MY SUMMER PROJECT FOR SCHOOL WAS GOING TO BE AN INSECT COLLECTION...
うう う...
BUT THERE'S JUST TOO MUCH COMPETITION IN THE CITY...
GUESS I SHOULD CHANGE TOPICS...
BUT THERE'S NOT MUCH TIME LEFT BEFORE IT'S DUE!

古和医院
田中商店
営業中
お食事処
?
THAT'S ...
お食事処
かおる
THAT'S IT!!

HAVE A SEAT!
お食事処
電話番号
THIS IS HIS HABITAT...
...
A REPORT ON THE DAILY LIFE OF A PENGUIN... WHAT A GREAT IDEA!
IF I DO GOOD ON THIS REPORT, MAYBE I'LL GET ACCEPTED INTO A PRESTIGIOUS MIDDLE SCHOOL...!
...
THERE'S A LOT RIDING ON THIS!
I BETTER GIVE IT MY ALL!!
SO, WHAT'S THE PENGUIN DOING NOW--?
GASP!
!

HE'S EATING FRIED SHRIMP!!
ポーン
AND DOING TRICKS?!
SNATCH
WOW...
......
トコ トコトコ
CREAK
A TOILET TRAINED PENGUIN ?!
御手洗
し〜ん
(REST ROOM)
FLUSH
No way!!!!
HE EVEN FLUSHED!!

UMM.. ARE YOU OKAY? YOU LOOK PALE...
HUH?
ARE YOU ALL RIGHT? ARE YOU SICK?
I'M OKAY ...
She's hot!
Klunk
I WAS JUST SUR-PRISED BY THE PENGUIN ...
BUT I'M FINE!
OH, DID GIN-CHAN SCARE YOU?
HEY, GIN! CAN YOU GO BUY SOME DAIKON RADISHES? I'M ALL OUT!
SQUAWK!!
SH-SHOP-PING--?

イリエ
商店街
(IRIE SHOPPING DISTRICT)
トコ トコ
トコ
A SHOPPING PENGUIN...?
HEY! IT'S THE GINSTER!!
GOT SOME NICE SARDINES IN! WANT SOME?
GIN-CHAN!
手作りカップ
GIN! GOT TIME TO CHAT?
肉
HE'S SO POPULAR...
GIN-CHAN! YOU'RE SO CUTE!!

八百八
HOW'YA DOING, GIN?
WE JUST HAD A DELIVERY THIS MORNING! EVERYTHING'S FRESH!!
DAIKON RADISHES? THOSE ARE REALLY GOOD!
.....
THEY'RE REAL FIRM, AND NICE AND WHITE! PRETTY GOOD FOR THE SUMMER CROP!
ONLY ¥100 A PIECE!!
WHAT?!
GLARE
...
WHAT'S THAT LOOK?
It's too expensive, huh?
HOW ABOUT ¥75...?

.....
GLARE
.....
FINE! TAKE 'EM FOR ¥10 A PIECE, THEN...
SQUAWK!
八百八
HE GOT ALL THAT FOR 40 YEN?!
He stared him down to 90 percent off?
SALE
HE MUST BE ABLE TO UNDER-STAND HUMAN LAN-GUAGE...
メモ メモ...
WHAT NOW?
....

GASP!
結局南極
気分爽快!!
ボォ~!
COOL MINT
...
HE'S STARING AT THAT SEXY POSTER!!
ガーン!
NOW HE'S MOVING CLOSER TO IT!
THAT'S ONE PERVERTED PENGUIN!!
トコ
トコ
BUT HE LOOKS SO CUTE AND INNOCENT!!
HEY, WAIT A MINUTE ...

THAT'S THE SOUTH POLE...
PHEW!
I GUESS HE'S JUST HOME-SICK...
.....
...
BUT...
...HE SURE DOES HAVE A SLIMY LOOK ON HIS FACE...
HE'S A PERVERT AFTER ALL!!
WELL, I'M NOT GOING TO BE FOOLED BY THAT CUTE AND INNOCENT ACT!!
CLENCH!

GIN-CHAN, IT'S BATH TIME!!
SQUAWK!!
お食事処
カポ～ン..
.....
COLD WATER BATHS ARE THE BEST CURE FOR THIS SUMMER HEAT!!
...
.....
ぷか～.

I-I'M NOT REALLY BEING A PEEPING PERVERT...
I'M ONLY DOING THIS FOR MY SCIENCE PROJECT!
BUT THAT DARN PENGUIN IS IN THE WAY!!
GRRRR!
MOVE!! YOU STUPID PEN-GUIN!!
TIME TO WASH, GIN-CHAN!
!
...
WASH... THAT MEANS...
...SHE'S GOING TO STAND UP...
...
!
UMF!
...

HEY! IS SOMEONE UP ON MY ROOF?!!
GASP!!
WHO'S OUT THERE?!

...
UH...
.....
HI...
HI, MINAKO...
DON'T CATCH A COLD...
Bye now!!
WHAT...
WHAT'RE YOU DOING OUT THERE, DAD?!!
...
OUCH!

PHEW! THAT WAS CLOSE...
ALMOST GOT CAUGHT...
BUT I GOT PLENTY OF GOOD INFO FOR MY REPORT!
THIS IS GOING TO BE GREAT!
観察ノート
Campus
(PENGUIN OBSERVATION NOTEBOOK)
MY SUMMER SCIENCE PROJECT WILL PROVE TO MY CLASS AND THE WORLD THAT...
...PEN-GUINS AREN'T AS CUTE AND INNOCENT AS PEOPLE THINK THEY ARE!!!
THEN THEY'LL HAVE TO ACCEPT ME INTO A PRESTIGIOUS MIDDLE SCHOOL!

THE NEW SEMESTER...
キンコーン
キンコーン
.....
DO YOU REALLY EXPECT ME...
...TO TAKE THIS REPORT SERI-OUSLY?

EVERYONE IS BEING DECEIVED!!
WHAT PENGUINS ARE REALLY LIKE!
*refer to notebook and photographs for more detail!!
Penguin eyes have the power to make the man at the produce stand cry!
Penguins are intelligent! They appear to understand human language!!
A penguin's diet consists mainly of fried shrimp! But, they don't seem to be very picky eaters.
PENGUINS ARE PER-VERTED!!!
(see attached photo for genuine proof!)
Penguins are fashion conscious! This one always wears a black tie!
*
PENGUINS ARE TOILET TRAINED!!
(They even flush!!!)
アハハ
OUCH!
WHAT WERE YOU THINK-ING?!
WHAT KIND OF SCIENCE PROJECT IS THIS?
BUT IT'S TRUE...

CHAPTER 8
THE MYSTERY EGG

.....
IT'S MORNING...
チュン
チュン
食事処
THE RESTAURANT'S ABOUT TO OPEN...
IT'S SO UNLIKE MINAKO TO OVERSLEEP...
.....
ボォ〜〜
IT'S MORNING, MINAKO!!
TIME TO WAKE--

チュン
UNH...
MMH...
チュン...
HUH?
AN EGG?

SQUAWK?!
Egg
MINAKO LAID AN EGG?!!
GASP!
ALL DONE!

W-W-WHO DID IT?!
WHO'S THE FATHER?!!
NO! NO!
WHO DID THIS TO MY MINAKO?!!
NO! NO! NO!
OH NO!!!!
WAIT A SEC...
HUH?!
.....
THAT'S NOT POSSIBLE...
Minako's human. She can't lay an egg...
It's so huge...
BUT THEN... WHO COULD HAVE...
...LAID THIS EGG...?
つるん...
?
ムク...
MM... WHAT'S THE MATTER, GIN-CHAN ...?

KYAAAA!!
SQUAWK!!
GIN-CHAN! YOU LAID AN EGG!!
WHAT?!
GIN-CHAN... YOU'RE A FEMALE!
NO, I'M NOT!!!
YOU LAID SUCH A HUGE AND PERFECT EGG!! IT'S BEAUTIFUL!!
SQUAWWK!!

I WONDER WHO THE FATHER IS...
THERE IS NO FATHER!!
I KNOW! IT'S THAT FUNNY LITTLE PENGUIN WITH THE BOW TIE!
MIKE?!
FWUMP
NO WAY!!!!!
HEY! NOW THAT I KNOW YOU'RE A GIRL...
WE HAVE TO CHANGE YOUR WARD-ROBE!
I'M A MAN!!
DON'T BE EMBAR-RASSED!!
It's only natural!
.....

TADAA!!
.....
mutter mutter mutter
APPEARANCE IS IMPORTANT FOR A LADY!
.....
mutter mutter
MY DOLL'S CLOTHES FIT YOU PERFECTLY!
うんうん
I HAVE A LOT MORE, TOO!
WE'RE GOING TO HAVE SO MUCH FUN!!
.....
WHAT AM I...?
...A MAN...? OR A WOMAN...?

GIN-CHAN, NOW THAT YOU'RE GOING TO BE A MOTHER...
YOU HAVE TO BE RESPONSIBLE AND TAKE CARE OF YOURSELF!
.....
MOTHERHOOD
......
...I'M A... WOMAN...
...

I'M OFF TO SCHOOL NOW!
I'LL COME STRAIGHT HOME TODAY! OKAY, GIN-CHAN?
お食事処
かおる
YOU JUST LAID AN EGG, SO BE SURE AND EAT PROPERLY TODAY, OKAY?
Good girl, good girl.
.....
MINAKO ...
YOU'RE ROBBING ME OF MY MASCU-LINITY...
Bye, Gin-chan!
.....
GASP!!
I'M INSTINC-TIVELY INCU-BATING THE EGG!
MAYBE I REALLY AM FEMALE...

I SEE THAT YOUR EGG IS PRECIOUS TO YOU!
MIKE!!
MIKE, DID I REALLY LAY THIS EGG?!
WHAT ARE YOU TALKING ABOUT, BOSS? MALE PENGUINS DON'T LAY EGGS!!
SO I AM MALE, RIGHT ...?
OF COURSE YOU ARE!!
BOSS...
YOU'RE NOT THAT EGG'S MOTHER, YOU'RE ITS FATHER!
HUH?!
Its father...?
THAT'S RIGHT. AND...
LINDA! C'MON OUT!
!!

ひょこん..
.....
SHUF
SHUF
A PINK PENGUIN ?!
LINDA DYES HER FEATHERS FOR SHOW BUSINESS!
AND BOSS, IT WAS *YOU* THAT MADE LINDA...
...LAY THAT EGG!!
HUG
.....
GASP!
...
pat pat

I DELIVERED THAT EGG TO YOU, BOSS!
WIPE WIPE
BOTH THE MAMA PENGUIN AND THE PAPA PENGUIN TAKE TURNS TO KEEP THE EGG WARM.
DUHH...
IT'S A PENGUIN PARENTS' DUTY!!
BUT LINDA'S BEEN INCUBATING THE EGG ALL BY HERSELF... SHE HASN'T EVEN HAD TIME TO EAT!
.....
BOSS, YOU'VE ABANDONED LINDA IN HER TIME OF NEED...
I REALLY CAN'T BELIEVE YOU...
.....
GRRR
SNAP

YOU'RE GIVING ALL OF US COCKS A BAD NAME!
YOU'VE GOT TO TAKE RESPON-SIBILITY FOR YOUR ACTIONS!
GASP!
HUH?
.....
WAIT A MINUTE, MIKE!!
BOSS, YOU ALWAYS MANAGE TO OUTDO US...
LINDA IS OUR BELOVED IDOL! WE ALL LOVE HER!

...
LINDA SAYS SHE'S CHERISHED THE MEMORY OF THAT DAY AND IT'S BEEN HER REASON FOR LIVING...
WHISPER WHISPER
...
IT JUST CAN'T BE! NOTHING EVER HAPPENED!!
YOU JUST HAD A FIGHT WITH THE OLD BOSS, AND YOU WERE IN PRETTY BAD SHAPE...
AND THAT WAS WHEN YOU APPROACHED LINDA!
Flower garden
UGHH...
drip drip
AND THEN YOU...
FWOM
?
MIKE, I HAVE TO TELL YOU SOMETHING...
FWUMP
YOU TOOK ADVANTAGE OF HER!!
MIKE, YOU IDIOT! I JUST FAINTED AND LANDED ON TOP OF HER!

MIKE, LISTEN TO ME...
I'M ACTUALLY A HUMAN!
SO THERE'S REALLY NO WAY I WOULD BE AROUSED BY A PENGUIN!!
Gin-Chan!
BESIDES, MINAKO IS THE ONLY TRUE LOVE OF MY LIFE!
BUT, BOSS, YOU SURE DO LOOK LIKE A PENGUIN TO ME!
What a feeble lie!!
I'M TRYING TO TELL YOU THAT--
I WON'T BE FOOLED BY YOUR LAME EXCUSES! AFTER ALL, I'M A GENIUS!!
ARRGH! IT'S NOT AN EXCUSE!!
OH, BOSS, STOP TRYING TO MAKE FOOLS OF US!!

KII KII KIIII!!
バッ!
GASP!
WHAT THE --?!
YOU HURT HER FEELINGS, BOSS!!
HEY! WHERE'RE YOU GOING?!
ペタ
ペタ
ペタ
危険である
YOU SAID ALL THOSE CRUEL THINGS ABOUT LINDA! YOU BETTER GO APOLOGIZE!
!
WHAT THE--?!

KII! KII! KII!
WHOA!
!
FWUMP!
BOSS!
CRAZY LINDA! HOW COULD YOU DO THAT TO YOUR OWN EGG?!
BUT, YOU DROVE HER TO THIS MADNESS, BOSS!!
くらっ
ARRRGH

BOSS, YOU CAN'T RUN AWAY FROM THAT EGG ANYMORE!
BE A COCK AND TAKE RESPONSI-BILITY FOR YOUR ACTIONS!!
DARN YOU...
MIKE...
.....
smirk

.....
HUH...
.....
MINAKO! YOU'RE HOME A BIT LATE TODAY!
HELLO!
AHHH!
A P-PINK PENGUIN ...?
AAAH...

THAT'S RIGHT!
THAT PINK PENGUIN IS GIN'S WIFE!
THEN SHE LAID THAT EGG?!
AHHH!
.....
Cut it out!
SNATCH
MNCH MNCH
HEY, GIN!! YOUR WIFE CAME ALL THIS WAY TO VISIT!
YOU BE NICE TO HER!!
WIFE?!

WE CAN'T LEAVE YOU ALONE FOR A MINUTE, GIN-CHAN!
YOU'VE GOT SUCH A PRETTY LITTLE WIFE! AND A BRAND NEW BEAUTIFUL EGG, TOO!
MINAKO IT'S NOT TRUE!!!

CHAPTER 9
EYEWITNESS...

チュン
チュン...
NNF! WHAT A BEAUTIFUL MORNING !!
SQUAWK...
FROM TODAY, MIKE AND LINDA WILL BECOME MEMBERS OF THE RESTAURANT KAORU HOUSEHOLD...
HUH?!
お食事処 かお
SOMETHING...
...SMELLS HORRIBLE...
What is this stench..?
IT'S COMING FROM INSIDE THE BED...
ぷ〜ん
...?
IS THAT A FISH-TAIL?
そお〜〜っと..
...

TISSUE
SQUAWK!!
WHA--!?!!
.....
くが〜...
ZZZZ
...FOR THE RESTAURANT...
OUR STOCK OF FISH...
ZZZZ
DARNIT! LINDA BROUGHT FOOD INTO BED!!
SQUAWK!

WHY DID YOU HAVE TO PUT ALL THAT FISH IN MY BED?! NOW MY ENTIRE BODY SMELLS LIKE FISH!!
SQUAWK! THIS WATER IS SO WARM!
......
.....
AT THIS RATE, I WON'T BE ABLE TO HELP OUT TODAY...
I HOPE DAD CAN HANDLE THINGS BY HIMSELF...
I'LL HAVE TO CLEAN THE SLIME OFF THE FLOORS AND THEN WASH THE FUTON AND MY PAJAMAS...
HM? ARE YOU APOLOGIZING? HOW CUTE!
DON'T WORRY. I'M NOT MAD ANYMORE.
RUB RUB
OKAY, IT'S THE NEXT PEN-GUIN'S TURN!
DARN IT...

(SUPER TOXIC RUST REMOVER)

チュ〜ッ
squirt squirt
MUTTER
MUTTER
MAYBE I REALLY AM THE FATHER OF THAT EGG? I'M BEGINNING TO WONDER...
MUTTER
ピッ
HUH?
OH NO! GIN-CHAN!!
LINDA! YOU CAN'T WASH GIN-CHAN'S BACK WITH A STEEL BRUSH!!
AH...
TWITCH
GIN'S HAVING SEIZURES OF PAIN...
TWITCH
UGH...
TWITCH
オロオロ

.....
お食事処
IT'S BEEN A PRETTY TOUGH MORNING FOR US, HASN'T IT?
.....
.....
TREMBLE TREMBLE
.....
I HAVE TO GET TO SCHOOL, NOW... YOU ALL BETTER BE GOOD...
DON'T GET INTO ANY MORE TROUBLE!
ガラッ
Bye now!
.....

HUG!!
RUB RUB
~!!
YARGHH!!
?
NNN...
WHAT'S THE BIG IDEA?!
SQUAWK!!
AND QUIT POINTING YOUR UGLY BEAK AT ME!
.....
L-LINDA!!
HMPH!
ドスッ
JEEZ...
.....

BOSS!! HOW CAN YOU BE SO MEAN TO LINDA?!
WHAT DO YOU KNOW?! THERE'S PAIN THAT I CAN DEAL WITH AND THEN THERE'S REAL PAIN!
YOU'RE PLANNING TO KICK LINDA OUT AND SHIRK YOUR RESPONSIBILITIES!!
I know what you're up to!
I TOLD YOU...
御用
I WOULD NEVER MATE WITH A PENGUIN BECAUSE I'M A HUMAN ON THE INSIDE!!
HOW DUMB DO YOU THINK LINDA AND I ARE?! YOU CAN'T LIE TO US LIKE THAT!!
CRASH
Gasp!
WHAT WAS THAT?!
It came from the kitchen!

mnch
mnch
mnch
...?
LINDA'S TRYING TO EAT HER WORRIES AWAY!
SHE'S EATEN EVERY-THING DOWN TO THE LAST SQUID...
THAT DOES IT... GET OUT!
WHAT?!
mnch
mnch
BOTH OF YOU! GET OUT OF THIS HOUSE!!
.....
OOPS ...
FORGOT TO GIVE THEM THE EGG...

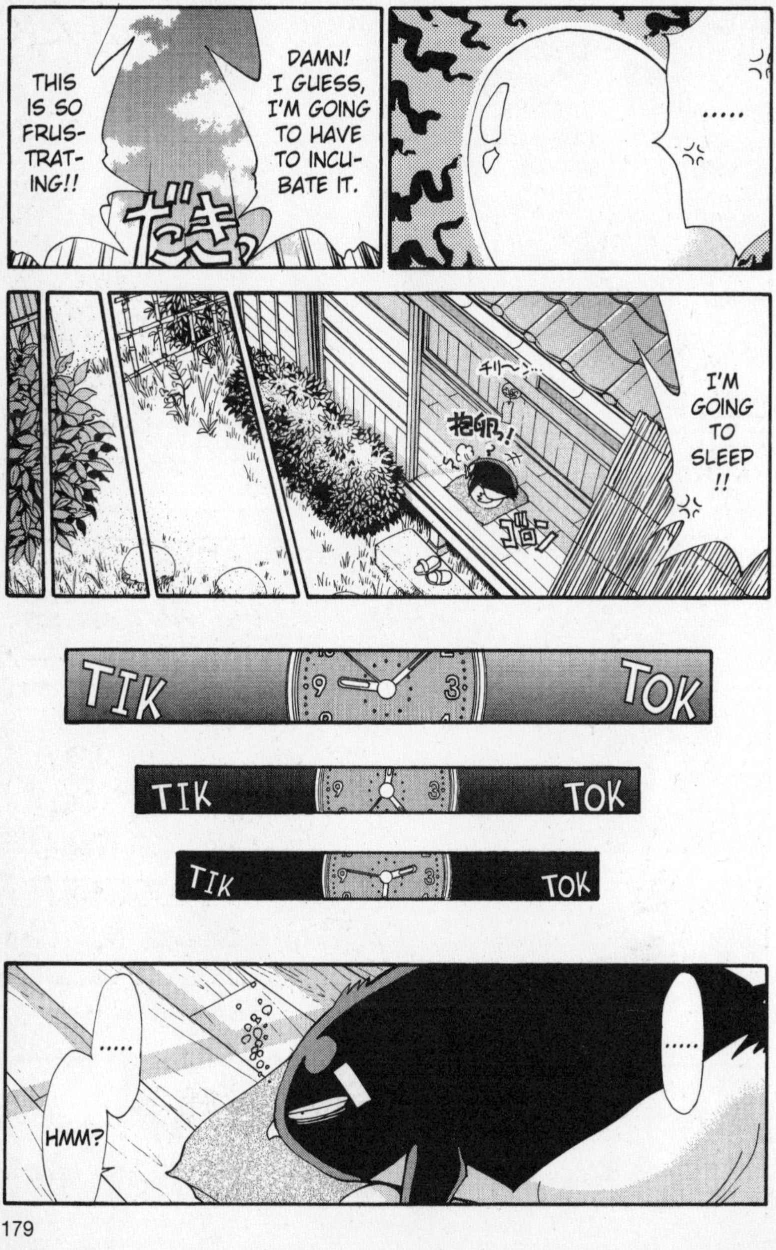
DAMN! I GUESS, I'M GOING TO HAVE TO INCUBATE IT.
THIS IS SO FRUS-TRAT-ING!!
.....
I'M GOING TO SLEEP !!
TIK
TOK
TIK
TOK
TIK
TOK
.....
.....
HMM?

ミィ～ンミィ～ン
ス～ス～
WHA--?!
Gasp!
びっくり..
ス～...
ス～
MINAKO... WHEN DID YOU GET HOME?
I'VE BEEN SLEEPING FOR QUITE A WHILE...
IT'S ALREADY EVENING.
TIK TOK
TIK TOK

BUT WHY IS SHE SLEEPING HERE...?
I GUESS SHE MUST BE TIRED. AFTER ALL, SHE WENT STRAIGHT TO SCHOOL AFTER CLEANING UP ALL THAT FISH...
IT'S ALL THEIR FAULT...
THOSE TWO HAVE BEEN NOTHING BUT TROUBLE...
GULP!
...
MAYBE I SHOULD COVER HER UP WITH A BLANKET.
リ〜ン
くるっ…

I THINK THE EXTRA BLANKETS ARE IN THE LIVING ROOM CLOSET...
LINDA!
...
YOU NEED TO FORGET ABOUT THE BOSS!!
HE KEEPS LYING ABOUT LIKING THAT HUMAN GIRL EVEN THOUGH HE'S A PENGUIN...
A GUY LIKE THAT CAN'T MAKE YOU HAPPY!
.....
LET'S GO BACK TO THE AQUAR-IUM...
AND...
IF YOU DON'T MIND...
UM... I... UH... *I'LL* BE THE FATHER OF THAT EGG!
I... I... PROMISE TO MAKE YOU HAPPY!!
I'LL TREAT YOU MUCH BETTER THAN THE BOSS...
!

!
...?
...
AND I PROMISE THAT I'LL--
!!

スゥ..
.....
!
ガーン!
THERE'S NO WAY I WOULD MATE WITH YOU!
MINAKO IS MY TRUE LO--

.....
OOPS, WHAT AM I DOING?
...
I SHOULD WAIT UNTIL I TURN BACK INTO A HUMAN TO KISS MINAKO...
patience patience
...
トボトボ
WHAT'S WRONG, LINDA?!
Weren't you listening to me?
.....
GASP!
I'M SORRY, LINDA... I DIDN'T MEAN TO GET YOU MAD...

PHEW...
THAT WAS A NICE BATH!
お食事処
DAMN!
GRR! GRR!
IF MY BACK WASN'T ALL SCRATCHED UP, I WOULD'VE BEEN ABLE TO TAKE A BATH WITH MINAKO!!
HMM...
...
munch munch
...
WHAT'S GOING ON IN HERE? WHY IS EVERYONE SO GLUM?

WHAT'S THE MATTER, LINDA...?
!
.....
EVERY-ONE'S IN BAD A MOOD...
hmm...
GIN-CHAN... YOU SHOULD BE NICER TO LINDA.
She's mad...
FUp
GASP!
!
OUCH!!

HUH?
PENGUIN
PENGUIN
OWWW...
drip
WHAT'S...
ouch!
WHAT'S GOING ON HERE...?

In the original Japanese editions, TUXEDO GIN has the sub-title, Ginji no Koi no Monogatari. Literally translated, it means "The story of Ginji's love." But, the sub-title also pays comic tribute to a classic karaoke song popular with middle-aged men entitled, Ginza no Koi no Monogatari. Recorded in 1962 by actor Yujiro Ishihara (brother of controversial Governor of Tokyo, Shintaro Ishihara) and Junko Makimura, the title literally means "Ginza love story." Check in next volume for more gleanings on aquatic birds, transmogrification, and near death experiences.

Glossary of Sound Effects, Signs, and other Miscellaneous Notes

Each entry includes: the location, indicated by page number and panel number (so 3.1 means page 3, panel number 1); the phonetic romanization of the original Japanese; and our English "translation"—we offer as close an English equivalent as we can.

CHAPTER 2

26.1——FX: SAN SAN (sunny)
26.1——FX: MIIIIN MIIIIN (cicada)
26.2——FX: PACHA PACHA (splattering water)
27.1——FX: JIRI JIRI (hot)
27.1——FX: BASHA BASHA (splattering water)
28.1——FX: BURAN (dangling)
28.3——FX: CHIRIIN (wind chime)
29.1——FX: CHIRIIN (wind chime)
29.3——FX: WAAAAN (crying)
31.3——FX: SHIIIIN (silence)
32.2——FX: KOTU KOTU (walking)
32.4——FX: KUHAHAHAHA (laughter)
32.5——FX: UHIHI... (laugh)
33.2——FX: BI (fwip)
34.1——FX: ZAZAZAZAZA (things moving)
34.2——FX: GOGOGOGO (roar)
35.1——FX: GON (smack)
35.3——FX: ZUDON! (thunk)
35.4——FX: GON (bam!)
36.1——FX: PYON (hop)
37.1——FX: DOKA DOKA DOKA (bump bump bump)
37.2——FX: ZABABABA (splash splash)
38~39.1-FX: GAYA GAYA (loudness)
38~39.1-FX: ZAWA ZAWA ZAWA (crowding)
38~39.3-FX: SHUUU (smoking)
40.1——FX: DODON! (firework exploding)
40.2——FX: PAPARA (fireworks)
40.2——FX: KUWA (squawk)
42.2——FX: GARA (opens door opening)
43.2——FX: WAA!! (crowd noise)
43.2——FX: PI PI (whistle)

CHAPTER 1

8.1——sign: Oshokuji Dokoro Kaoru (Restaurant Kaoru)
8.2——FX: MOGU MOGU (chewing)
8.2——sign: Tezukuri Ice Candy (homemade popsicles)
11.4——FX: BOOOO (daydreaming)
11.5——FX: BOOO (daydreaming)
12.1——sign: Tezukuri Ice Candy (homemade popsicles)
——sign: 1 pon 300 yen (1 for 300)
12.2——FX: CHI (clicks tongue)
14.4——FX: ZUZUUUN (standing up tall)
15.3——FX: BAN (jump)
16.1——FX: DOKA (bam)
16.2——FX: KURA (dizzy)
16.3——FX: PASHIIN! (smack!)
16.4——FX: BAIN! (bump)
16.5——FX: PAIIN (smack)
16.6——FX: PIKI (twitch)
17.4——FX: ZAWA ZAWA ZAWA (crowd noise)
17.5——FX: WAI WAI GAYA GAYA (loud crowd)
18.4——FX: WAAAA (crowd cheering)
19.1——FX: ZAPAAAN (sound of waves)
20.1——FX: HARARI (paper falls off)
21.4——FX: ZAZAAAN (sound of waves)
22.1——FX: BAAAN! (dramatic posing)
22.1——FX: ZAZAZAZA (sound of waves)
22.2——FX: PETA PETA PETA (flop flop)
23.1——FX: BOCHA (wet falling sound)
24.2——FX: SHIIIN (silence)
24.6——[Originally the boy says, "Look mom, a Tanuki-man!" referring to Musashi's swollen testes. Tanuki are a breed of a raccoon-like dog revered as a sort of deity of food and drink. Statues of tanuki with disproportionately large testes are commonly displayed outside restaurants and drinking establishments in Japan to beckon customers in.]

CHAPTER 4

66.1——FX: MIIN MIIN (cry of cicada)

66.2——FX: MIIIN (cicada)

67.1——FX: HYOUU (wind)

69.1——FX: BAN (boom)

70.1——FX: DA (dashes off)

74.5——FX: DODODODO (machinery)

74.5——FX: BABABABA (machinery)

74.5——FX: GARA GARA (rattle rattle)

76.1——signs: Kawatetsu (a name); Maguro Senmon (Specializing in Tuna)

77.2——FX: ZURI ZURI (dragging self)

77.2——FX: FURA FURA (staggering)

78.3——FX: BAAN (zoom)

79.6——FX: ZA (steps)

82.2——FX: BAFU (collapses onto bed)

82.5——FX: GORON (rolls over)

83.2——FX: KAAAA (turning red)

83.2——FX: HAHA (laugh)

83.2——FX: DOKI DOKI (heart)

84.1——FX: KUU KUU (sleep)

CHAPTER 5

86.1——sign: Oshokujidokoro Kaoru (Restaurant Kaoru)

86.4——FX: DONDONDON KARAKAKKA (drum sounds)

87.1——FX: DONDONDON KARAKAKKA (drum sounds)

87.2——FX: DODONGADON (drums)

87.2——FX: GAYA GAYA (crowd)

87.3——FX: FUFUN (good mood)

88.1——FX: BOOOO (daydreaming)

88.2——FX: PORO (cigarette ash falls)

88.2——FX: GOKU... (swallows saliva)

88.2——FX: JIIII (staring)

89.1——FX: DON DON DON (drums)

89.4——FX: ZUI (coming closer)

43.2——FX: GUWA GUWA GUWA (penguins squawks)

43.3——FX: TA TA TA (running)

43.5——FX: KAPO (puts hat on)

44.1——FX: WAAAAAAAA (crowd)

CHAPTER 3

47.3——FX: CHA (raises fishing pole)

47.3——FX: PATA PATA (lure flapping)

47.4——FX: HYUN HYUN (swinging pole)

48.1——FX: GAAN (shocked)

49.2——FX: TOKO TOKO TOKO (walking)

50.3——FX: SHIIIN (silence)

50.4——FX: KUN! (bob)

50.5——FX: BI (pulls)

51.1——FX: BICHIIN (slap)

52.1——FX: BO (flare)

52.1——FX: SUPA SUPA (puff puff)

52.2——FX: MOGU (munch)

53.4——FX: PACHA PACHA (splashes)

54.3——FX: SUIII (swims over)

55.5——FX: SHUBA! (swing)

56.1——FX: PACHA (splash)

56.2——FX: CHIKI CHIKI (reeling)

56.3——FX: YURA (floating)

56.4——FX: GATSUN (pull)

57.1——FX: BAKIN (breaks)

59.1——FX: BA (jump)

59.2——FX: BIIN (tension on line)

59.3——FX: GIRI GIRI (tension)

60.1——FX: ZUPOON (big splash)

63.2——FX: DAAAAAHAHA (big laugh)

64.2——FX: DOTA DOKA BOKA SUKA BATA (struggling)

64.3——FX: KAPOOON (echo)

111.1—FX: GORO GORO (roll roll)

111.5—FX: SUTA... (walking)

112.1—FX: BOSO (mumbles)

112.2—FX: GATA GATA (rattle)

112.3—FX: SU (shuf)

112.4—FX: GASA GOSO (rustle rustle)

113.1—FX: BISHI (snapping rope tight)

113.4—FX: GOO (wind)

113.4—sign: Oshokujidokoro Kaoru (Restaurant Kaoru)

114.1—FX: GOO (wind)

114.2—FX: HYUOO (wind)

115.1—FX: KUKUKU (laughing)

115.4—FX: KUUU (crying)

115.5—FX: HYUU (wind)

116.1—FX: BYUUU (wind)

117.1—FX: GOGOGO (roar)

117.2—FX: KURU (fwip)

117.4—FX: GOOO (wind)

117.6—FX: SOOO (inching out)

118.1—FX: GOOOO (roar)

118.2—FX: DAA! (dash)

119.1—FX: SHAKI (raises hands in panic)

121.1—FX: BA (fwoosh)

121.2—FX: SHUOO (fwoosh)

122.1—FX: GOOOO... (roar)

122.1—FX: DOKA (crash)

122.2—FX: GAAAAN (shock)

124.1—FX: ZAAAA (rain)

124.3—FX: MUKU (gets up)

124.5—FX: JIN JIN (throb)

125.2—FX: PORO PORO (crying)

126.1—FX: MIIIN MIIN (cicada)

126.2—FX: MIIIIIIN MIIIIIN (cicada)

90.1—sign: Anzu Ame (Apricot Candy)

91.2—FX: KARI KARI KARI KARI (scratch scratch)

91.2—FX: SHIIIN (silence)

92.2—FX: CHARI (chak)

94.3—FX: KARAN KORON (footsteps of wooden sandals)

95.4—FX: GYU (hug)

96.4—FX: DON (bump)

96.5—FX: ZA (falling to ground)

96.5—FX: DOSA (being dumped on ground)

97.3—FX: GU (grabs hand)

99.1—FX: DOKAN (thwak)

99.3—FX: BAGA (falls to ground)

100.1—FX: GUGU (clenches fist)

100.1—FX: KUAAAAAA (cry)

100.2—FX: DOKA DOGA GASU (kick stomp etc)

101.1—FX: BAAAAAN (taking position)

102.1—FX: DA! (running)

102.3—FX: BATTARI (falls)

102.4—FX: BAAN (takes position)

103.1—FX: BABABABABA (punches)

103.2—FX: BASU DOKA ZUN (stabbing, hitting noise)

104.2—FX: KARAN KORON (wooden sandal steps)

105.1—FX: WAHAHA (big laugh)

105.2—FX: SHIIIIN (silence)

105.4—FX: PIKU! (perking up)

CHAPTER 6

110.1—FX: BYUO (strong wind)

110.1—sign: Oshokujidokoro Kaoru (Restaurant Kaoru)

110.2—FX: GATA GATA (rattle rattle)

110.2—FX: HYUU (wind)

110.4—FX: CHIRIIIN (bell)

CHAPTER 7

129.1 —FX: CHIRIIIN (ring)

129.3—FX: ZA (fwip)

129.4—FX: ZUZA! (fwip)

129.5—FX: BIKUUU! (startled)

130.1 —FX: DA! (dash)

130.2—FX: DAA! (dash)

130.2—FX: HYUU (post stampede draft)

130.3—FX: UUU... (sob)

131.3—sign: Oshokujidokoro Kaoru (Restaurant Kaoru)

131.4—FX: BAN (determination)

132.1 —sign: Oshokujidokoro Kaoru (Restaurant Kaoru)

132.2—FX: GOKURI (gulp)

132.3—FX: KACHA KACHA (klanking dishes)

133.1 —FX: GATA (falling out of seat)

133.1 —FX: PON (toss)

133.4—FX: TOKO TOKO TOKO (waddle waddle)

133.5—FX: SHIIIIN (quiet)

134.3—FX: DOKI DOKI (heart beating)

134.4—FX: BI (raises hand)

135.2—FX: TOKO TOKO TOKO (walking)

137.4—FX: MEMO MEMO (writing notes)

138.1 —FX: BOOOO (dazed)

138.1 —poster: The poster is an advertisement for "Cool Mint Juice" with the catch phrase– "The feeling of the South Pole is so satisfying!"

138.2—FX: GAN! (shocked)

138.3—FX: TOKO TOKO (walking)

139.3—FX: BOOO (in a daze)

139.4—FX: UWAAA (crying)

140.2—FX: KAPON (splashy echo)

140.3—FX: PUKAA (floating)

141.1 —FX: PUKAA (floating)

141.2—FX: PACHA (splash)

141.3—FX: DOKI DOKI DOKI (heart beat)

141.4—FX: ZABA (splash)

141.5—FX: SOWA SOWA (glance glance)

141.6—FX: DOKI DOKI (heart beat)

141.7—FX: ZA (step)

142.1 —FX: DON! (shout)

142.3—FX: GARA (opens window)

144.1 —FX: ZURU ZURU (sliding down)

144.3—FX: GOGOGOGO (determination)

145.1 —FX: KINKON KINKON (school bell)

145.3—FX: PIKU (twitch)

146.2—FX: KAPON (hits with rolled up paper)

146.2—FX: AHAHAHA (other kids laughing)

146.3—FX: VUU (groaning)

CHAPTER 8

148.1 —FX: CHUN CHUN (birds chirping)

148.2—FX: BOOOO (sleepy)

148.3—FX: BA! (takes off comforter)

149.1 —FX: CHUN CHUN (chirp chirp)

150.1 —FX: BIKUN! (startled)

151.4—FX: TSURUN... (smooth and glimmering)

151.5—FX: MUKU (getting up)

152.1 —FX: DOKII (heart jumps)

152.2—FX: DON (dramatic fx)

153.4—FX: URI URI (poke poke)

154.5—Background: Characters for "Man?" and "Woman?" fill the background

155.3—Background: Character for "Woman" fills the background

156.4—FX: GAAN! (shocked)

157.1 —FX: TOKKO TOKKO (walking)

157.5 —FX: GYUUN! (turns around fast)

157.6 —FX: SHUBAA (swings arms)

158.1 —FX: HYOKON.. (popping out)

176.2—FX: ZUBABA (much pain)
176.4—FX: BIKU (startled)
176.6—FX: TOBO TOBO (walks off)
178.2—FX: KII! KII! (angry)
178.2—FX: KUCHA KUCHA (chewing)
178.4—FX: DOKA (boot)
178.5—FX: WANA WANA WANA (trembling in anger)
179.3—FX: CHIRIN (wind chime)
179.3—FX: HORAN (incubation)
179.3—FX: GORON (roll)
180.1—FX: SUU SUU (sleeping)
180.1—FX: MIIN MIIN (cry of cicada)
180.2—FX: BIKKURI… (surprised)
180.2—FX: SUU SUU (sleeping)
181.1—FX: SUU SUU (sleeping)
181.1—FX: CHIRIIN (wind chime)
181.5—FX: KURU (turns around)
181.5—FX: RIIIN (wind chime)
182.1—FX: GARA (opens door)
182.1—FX: TOKO TOKO (walking)
182.2—FX: PUN PUN (upset)
183.1—FX: RIRIIN (wind chime)
183.2—FX: KYORO KYORO (looks around)
183.4—FX: HYOKO (hops away)
183.4—FX: GUGU (stretching neck)
184.1—FX: SUU… (extending beak)
184.1—FX: GAAN! (shock)
184.3—FX: BIKU (startled)
185.1—FX: KU (getting up)
185.2—FX: TOBO TOBO (walking away weakly)
185.4—FX: GOGOGOGO (anger)
186.3—FX: ZUSSHIRI (tension)
187.2—FX: PUI (turns around)
188.1—FX: BAAN! (looking menacing)

158.3—FX: GAAN (shock)
159.3—FX: SUKU (gets up)
160.1—FX: BISHI! (points)
160.3—FX: GOSHI GOSHI (wiping drool)
160.3—FX: SUKU (gets up)
161.3—FX: FUN FUFUN! (humming)
163.1—FX: BA! (gets up)
163.3—FX: PETA PETA PETA (webbed feet running)
163.3—sign: Kiken de aru (danger)
163.4—FX: GABA (winding up for the throw)
164.1—FX: SHUBA! (throws)
164.1—FX: PASHI! (catch)
164.1—FX: TAN! (jump)
164.2—FX: DADA (runs to edge)
164.3—FX: PYUU (blood spurting out)
164.4—FX: KURA (losing consciousness)
166.4—FX: GURI GURI (shoving shrimp into face)
167.2—FX: URI URI (shoving shrimp)
168.2—FX: GAGAAAN (very shocked)

CHAPTER 9

170.1—FX: CHUN CHUN (chirp)
170.4—FX: PUUUN (stench)
170.6—FX: SOOTTO (slowly moving)
171.1—FX: PUUUUUUN (stench)
171.1—FX: KUKAAA (snoring)
172.1—FX: KAPOOON (splashy echo)
172.1—FX: GOSHI GOSHI GOSHI (scrub scrub scrub)
173.1—FX: JIIIII (stare)
173.3—FX: JIIIII (stare)
173.5—FX: KYORO KYORO (looking around)
174.1—FX: CHUU (squirt)
174.2—FX: PI (putting brush on Gin)
174.4—FX: ORO ORO (panicked)
175.5—FX: GARA (slides open door)

about manga artist,
Tokihiko Matsuura

Originally from Mie Prefecture, after working as an assistant for Tatsuya Egawa (GOLDEN BOY, TOKYO UNIVERSITY STORY), Matsuura made his manga artist debut in 1995 with WARP BOY in SHONEN SUNDAY. Other works include BRAVE SARU S ("Brave Monkey S") and RISING SUN.